MW01169604

When the Vow Breaks

Avoiding and overcoming the devastation of divorce

Thomas L. Smith

Copyright © 2016 Thomas L. Smith

All rights reserved.

ISBN:1539107264
ISBN-13: 978-1539107262

Dedication

County artist, Alan Jackson wrote and sings a song entitled "The Blues Man". In the lyrics of this song, Jackson sings,

"He did some things that messed up his thinking,
He was sure sinking, when she came along.
He was alone in the spotlight,
Not too much left in sight,
She changed all that one night
When she sang him this song.
Hey baby, I love you.

So I dedicate this book to my wife, Christy. She is the one, that God sent along, when I was sinking. If we are blessed in life, God sends someone to be a model of Jesus in our lives. To me, that is Christy. As I bring to close the most trying year of my life physically, after accidentally being shot in the stomach by a 40 caliber handgun in a firearms training class, Christy has loved me unconditionally. She has stood by my side, she has been a physician to my wounds, and has been a living example of Jesus himself. For which, I will forever be grateful. I dedicate this book to my children. They have modeled Jesus in forgiveness. Forgiveness of me taking them down a road called divorce. They never planned for this nor did they deserve it, yet they forgave. Jesus, Christy and my children are my reasons for living today, and for the remainder of my life.

FORWARD

Every pastor and family counselor will tell you that marriage difficulties are at an epidemic high. Relationship material is numerous at every bookstore, but where are the results in our families?

I have walked with author Tom Smith through his most hurtful, challenging and confusing years. Let him explain how he came out of his storm to help you. When your life is destroyed and in pieces, you must humble yourself and ask for a guide to help you recover.

This book is as real as it gets! In these pages you will discover your answers and receive your freedom. Time to dream again.

Pastor Glen Berteau
The House Modesto
Modesto, CA

CONTENTS

INTRODUCTION

Consider the words of someone who has been there:
"The effects of divorce as seen by one man."

"In the beginning I thought that if I could prove myself worthy she would consent to marry me. If I was a good provider, I thought , she won't have to work. But for all of this, when she tired of me, I will be driven out of my own home, made less welcome than a stranger. I was forbidden to come home, then told when I would be allowed to 'visit' my children.

Yes, God gave me children, but now I must prove my-self worthy to strangers to see them. I am forced to pay for them, whether or not these strangers allow me the privilege of seeing my children. And yes, the less they allow me to see them, the more they make me pay. If I object, even that privilege will be taken from me.

I won't be there for their first steps, first words, first tears, first bike rides, and even worse, I won't be there to prevent the first time they are possibly abused by another stranger perhaps living in my own home.

As for my wife, I am forced to continue to provide for her standard of living, so it doesn't fall. My standard of living is not considered unless I can't match her standard of living. Because I now live in poverty, the visitation rights that the strangers allowed me will be revoked because it would be 'harmful' for my children to visit my poverty. Yes, I said 'visit,' much like you show charity and visit a sick friend. Then when everything I have loved is gone. My children will call another man 'dad.' My wife sleeps with someone else, and I pay the bills. If I have any self-respect left it is only because they could not rip it out of me. All this I must accept with dignity because I am a man. And I am divorced."

This piece, written by a man I know, captures the emotional wallop of divorce. Some people say that divorce is liberating; an acceptable, even predictable end to a relationship that that no longer "serves my needs." I say, "Liberating? I don't think so." At least not any more liberating than am putative surgery.

I have interviewed many couples and individuals, victims of divorce, and will tell their stories, as well as some from my journey in the following pages. All of the accounts are true. These are real people, with real jobs, real lives, and we all still wrestle—even as you read this book—with the aftermath of divorce. Their names have been changed for obvious reasons.

You may notice that I call them victims. I do so because in divorce it seems everyone eventually becomes a victim. Victims of a selfish husband, victims of a selfish wife, victims of selfish parents, and victims of their own selfish desires. By "victim" I don't mean "blameless." Quite the opposite! I merely mean that everyone suffers, because divorce is like a hand grenade. If you're nearby, you're going to feel the shrapnel.

The Bible addresses and allows for divorce under certain conditions, and as we walk through the subject, we will address those conditions.

If you have been divorced, it is certainly not my intent to judge you. The Bible says in Romans 8:1, *There is therefore now no condemnation for those in Christ Jesus* (NIV). The purpose of this book is that you might never divorce again. If you have been divorced, you already know the unending sting divorce brings with it. If you have never been divorced, or are contemplating divorce, the purpose is to stop you from ruining your life and that of your family.

For those of you already headed for a shipwreck, there really is hope for you. Any and every marriage veering close to the rocky shores can be steered back into calm waters. David said in Psalm 73:46, *God is the strength of my heart.* (NIV). He didn't say "counseling sessions are the strength of my heart," though many people stake their lives on high-priced counselors. Neither did he say, "My husband/wife is the strength of my heart." They were never intended to be. The health of a marriage depends on one thing alone: Our love for God. He can restore, replace, renew and refresh even the most lifeless of covenants.

At times it takes a good deal of faith to believe he wants our marriage to survive. But he does, always and forever, not least because, as the senior partner in every marriage covenant, marriage hurts him most of all when it fails.

Oddly, most people don't consider divorce's effect on God. We think of him not as a person, but as a passionless caretaker. But—and this may shock you—God has emotions. He feels things. Any feeling you have ever had, God has felt infinitely deeper. Do you not believe me? I challenge you to reacquaint yourself with the God of the Bible. It doesn't take long to see that he is an emotional being. He loves us with a love we only barely understand.

He hates things that hurt us. He only desires good for us.

God hates divorce as passionately as he hates anything that gets between us and him. He created the human marriage covenant as a symbol of the ultimate union of Christ with the church. Indeed, our marriages are only a reflection of this. When we play around with this sacred relationship, behaving as if it doesn't matter to God or is none of his business, we desecrate the highest human covenant. We drag God's most prized relationship through the sewer.

God grieves deeply when man and woman are separated. He hurts more than either partner, because marriage isn't the union of two but of three, with God at the head. Divorce is betrayal of God. The prophet Malachi said this (we will return to portions of this Scripture in the next chapters):

Another thing you do: You flood the Lord's alter with tears. You weep and wail because he no longer pays attention to your offerings or accepts them with pleasure from your hands. You ask, 'Why?' It is because the Lord is acting as the witness between you and the wife of your youth, because you have broken faith with her, though she is your partner, the wife of your marriage covenant.

Has he not made them one? In flesh and spirit they are his. And why one? Because he was seeking godly offspring. So guard yourself in your spirit, and do not break faith with the wife of your youth. 'I hate divorce,' says the Lord God of Israel, 'and I hate a man's covering himself with violence as well as with his garment,' says the Lord Almighty. So guard yourself in your spirit, and do not break faith. (Malachi 2:13-16, NIV)

When we break faith with our partner, we break faith with God, and though he is a God of mercy, there are certain immutable laws that will always have consequences.

Severing a human relationship will have consequences as severe as severing a limb. There will be blood, There will be pain and wailing and untold misery.

In God there will be ultimate healing, but how much better not to waste countless years recuperation. How much better to take the shortcut to fullness by not breaking the faith of our youth, and not inviting the curse of divorce into our lives.

CHAPTER ONE

THE COVENANT...OR THE CURSE

The judge cracks the gavel against the hard wood one last time. The lawyers stand up and shake hands. The wife or the husband sits smugly, glad that they have "won" the biggest prize in the divorce settlement, while the other partner stews. The covenant that began in the shadow of the Cross has ended on the scales of justice. Yet the "victory" of this day is swallowed up in a hollow, echoing void. Both parties get up from their stiff, hard-backed chairs and walk through the grand doors of the divorce court, not quite sure that justice has been done today.

It seems to both the man and woman that the

word "finalized" bears a stinger that will poison them for the rest of their lives. It is a lie that their divorce will ever be final. They had waited for this day—"Finally, I can be released from her!" "Finally, that man will be out of my life and I can start afresh!" Now they know there's nothing final about it.

But, in truth the marriage's death knell came much earlier. No judge can disunite what God has united. No lawyer can persuade a spouse to abandon their mate for material gain. These people are merely functionaries, pallbearers who carry the coffin to the hole in the ground. They may take part in the burial—but they had nothing to do with the death.

In divorce, the marriage partners are the murder accomplices and the coroners of the lifelong covenant. An accomplice to murder doesn't always pull the trigger, but they do allow somebody to die unjustly. In marriage, we don't always take the knife and plunge it into the tender belly of our original covenant; sometimes circumstances or attacks from the devil form a wedge between us. Oftentimes both the man and the woman feel downright innocent as the blood flows.

But Jesus points to the marriage partners as responsible for divorce: *Moses permitted you to divorce your wives because your hearts were hard. But it was not this way from the beginning* (Matthew 19:8, NIV) The word of God further says this: *My flesh and my heart may fail, but God is the strength of my heart and my portion forever* (Psalm 73:46, NIV) The breaking of the marriage covenant is the result of a hard heart. Hearts become hard when their owners don't listen to God (see Pharaoh, for instance).

As a pastor and counselor, I can testify to the fatal potential of a hard heart: Every single person I have interviewed regarding divorce, myself included, has allowed his or her spirit to become hard. We rejected the truth of Scripture. We rejected the very advice of God, who created marriage. And when we reject God's instructions, the marriage machine always fails, leaving us with a dead partnership or divorce.

Divorce is not a matter for the lawyers and court clerks, though they make plenty of money off our failures. The seeds of divorce are sown and reaped in the human heart, where a harvest of bitterness, pain, and separation from God results. If we break our most sacred covenant with other humans, how much more difficult will it be to keep our sacred covenant with God? Far from the "fresh start" people hope for, divorce is more like saying, "I need a new car," then running the old one into a brick wall at 70 miles per hour before looking for a new one.

To understand how seriously God takes the breaking of the marriage covenant, we do well to look again at what we, as married people, promised in the beginning. After all, before there is divorce, there must first be a wedding. We know what a wedding looks like: The couple stands at the alter facing a pastor or priest bearing a bible and a beatific smile. The man and the woman beam at each other as the pastor speaks words like these:

"We are gathered here today to celebrate the happiest moment in the lives of these two people, for today they will affirm before witnesses in heaven and earth that they believe God has purposed that they covenant the remainder of their lives in the holy bonds of a Christian marriage. Sir, will you have this woman to be your wedded wife, to love and to live with after God's ordinances in the holy state of matrimony?" "I will."

"Will you love her, comfort her, honor her, and keep her in sickness and in health, forsaking all others, keeping yourself only unto her, as long as you both shall live?" "I will."

"Ma'am, will you have this man to be your wedded husband, to love and to live with after

God's ordinances in the holy state of matrimony?" "I will."

"Will you love him, comfort him, honor him, and keep him in sickness and in health, forsaking all others, keeping yourself only unto him, as long as you both shall live?" "I will."

"Will you take one another's hands and repeat after me? I, Joe, take you, Jane, to be my lawfully wedded husband/wife, to have and to hold, from this day forward, for better or worse, for richer or for poorer, in sickness and in health, to love and to cherish, forsaking all others, till death should part us. According to God's holy ordinances, I give you my all."

"What symbol of love have you brought? A ring. Would you both look at these rings. These rings are made in a circle, having no beginning or ending; they are a symbol of eternity; they are made of gold, the least tarnished and most enduring of the precious metals; they are to show how lasting and imperishable the covenant is that you are now mutually pledging.

Sir, would you place this ring on the fourth finger of your bride's left hand and repeat after me? With this ring, I thee wed. It is a visible affirmation of our love, and a token of the holy covenant we enter into today, with each other and with God.

Ma'am, would you place this ring on the fourth finger of your groom's left hand and repeat after me? With this ring, I thee wed. It is a visible affirmation of our love, and a token of the holy covenant we enter into today, with each other and with God.

Would you both repeat this together after me? May our love and our marriage be a shining reflection of Christ's love for His church and His people. Those whom God has joined together let no man put asunder.

For as much as these two people have covenanted together in holy wedlock, and it has been witnessed before God and this company, they have pledged their love to each other, and have declared the same by giving and receiving a ring. Being a minister of the gospel, I now pronounce that they are husband and wife, in the name of the Father, and the Son, and the Holy Spirit. Sir, you may kiss your wife. Ladies and gentlemen, may I present to you, Mr. and Mrs. Covenant-Maker!"

Did you notice a recurring word in that beautiful ceremony? I'll give you a hint: We almost never use it again after that blessed day is past. We instead use imperfect substitutes like "relationship," or "partnership," or "the ultimate in friendships." Certainly marriage is all of these things—but the word I'm looking for is "covenant."

One of the most significant problems we face when it comes to marriage is we prepare young couples for a wedding—and not for a covenant. When the ceremony ends, we close the Bible on the word and forget about it, seeking to build what we call "a relationship" with one another. Sure enough, a few months go by, and the relationship comes unmoored and drifts to sea because we have forgotten about the anchor of covenant.

God views marriage in a much, much deeper context than just a good relationship. Every covenant that God made with man is the Bible had consequences.

When the covenant was honored, the consequence was a blessing. When the covenant was broken, the consequence was a curse. This was God's covenant with Abraham, found in (Deuteronomy 11:24-28, NIV)

"Every place where you set your foot will be yours: your territory will extend from the desert to Lebanon, and from the Euphrates River to the Western Sea. No man will be able to stand against you. The Lord your God, as he promised you, will put the terror and fear of you on the whole land, wherever you go.

See, I am setting before you today a blessing and a curse—the blessing if you obey the commands of the Lord your God that I am giving you today; the curse if you disobey the commands of the Lord your God and turn from the way that I command you today by following other god's, which you have not known."

The blood covenant of old symbolizes much for marriages today, for God does not change. If we have changed and forgotten the meaning of covenant, that's our problem. How serious is God about a covenant? Extremely serious, as we'll see in the next chapter.

CHAPTER TWO

How does God view the Blood Covenant?

I have said the words hundreds of times: "Friends, we are gathered today to celebrate the happiest moments in the lives of these two people, for today they will affirm before witnesses in heaven and earth that they believe God has purposed that they covenant the remainder of their lives in the holy bonds of a Christian marriage." You know the scene is supposed to go after that: The cowboy rides off into the sunset with his new bride on the back of his favorite horse and they live happily ever after. The king chooses his queen and they live in the lavish palace on a hill in the kingdom all the days of their lives. Prince Charming comes as the answer to the poor country girl's prayer, sweeps her off the milk stool where she's in the middle of her chores, and takes hew away. Viola!

Happy endings are manufactured every day by film makers and storytellers. But, "happy" is not a word that goes well with "divorce." The last line of a romance novel where the fantasy couple is divorced would read something like this: "And so they were divorced, each going their separate ways leaving behind a trail of sorrows as they limped into a future marred by the fact that they had been ripped from their lifelong spiritual partner, broken the most solemn commitment they could make, and left behind a broken family that would never fully recover. The end."

Why is the pain of divorce so severe and violent? Could it be because it is a "breach of contract" with God? Remember (Malachi 2:16, NIV) *'I hate divorce,' says the Lord God of Israel, 'and I hate a man's covering himself with violence as well as with his garment,' says the Lord Almighty. So guard yourself in your spirit, and do not break faith.*

God is saying that divorce—the breaking of faith—covers a man with violence. The Hebrew language defines the word "violence" as "cruel injustice," "oppression," "violent dealings," and "damage." Anyone who has been through a divorce knows these words all too well. They describe an event in our personal lives as devastating as any violent physical attack.

Picture a bombed-out, gutted building where many have died in a terrorist strike. Not hard to imagine in the times we live today. Floors have collapsed in on each other at every level. Furniture is strewn across the piles of debris like dollhouse accessories. Internal bars and struts have been wrenched apart and dangle in mid-air like a compound fracture. The entire integrity of the building has been demolished.

Such is the picture of a person's life after divorce. Every insecurity is unleashed; every problem comes back to haunt the mind; every level of our personality collapses under the force of mutual betrayal. If people only displayed on the outside the effect divorce has on the inside, fewer people would consider it an option.

God says, I hate divorce because it covers a man with violence, as well as his garment. The Hebrew word for garment can be translated as "a robe" or "a wife." God hates divorce because it causes "cruel injustice," "oppression," "violent dealings," and "damage." To understand the violence divorce initiates, we need to understand the gravity of the covenant originally made with God and with one another.

"Covenant" is a good word, but it isn't mine—it's God's. God calls the marriage commitment a covenant, and the meaning and history of the word clue us into what God thinks of marriage. A covenant in the Old Testament was an agreement made between two parties, sealed in blood. God first instituted the blood covenant (of which marriage is a type) with Abram. Look at (Genesis 15:1-18, NIV)

After this, the word of the Lord came to Abram in a vision: 'Do not be afraid, Abram. I am your shield, your very great reward.' But Abram said, 'O sovereign Lord, what can you give me since I remain childless and the one who will inherit my estate is Eliezer of Damascus?' And Abram said, 'You have given me no children; so a servant in my household will be my heir.'

Then the word of the Lord came to him: 'This man will not be your heir, but a son coming from your own body will be your heir.' He took him outside and said, 'Look up at the heavens and count the stars—if indeed you can count them.' Abram believed the Lord, and he credited it to him as righteousness. He also said to him, 'I am the Lord, who brought you out of Ur of the Chaldeans to give you this land to take possession of it.' But Abram said, 'O sovereign Lord, how can I know that I will gain possession of it?'

So the Lord said to him, Bring me a heifer, a goat and a ram, each three years old, along with a dove and a young pigeon.' Abram brought all these to him, cut them in two and arranged the halves opposite each other; the birds, however, he did not cut in half.

When the sun had set and darkness had fallen, a smoking firepot with a blazing torch appeared and passed between the pieces. On that day the Lord made a covenant with Abram and said, 'To your descendants I give this land, from the river of Egypt to the great river, the Euphrates.'

Consider for a moment what happened here. For the covenant to be established, the animals to be offered were cut in halves, and arranged in proper order opposite one another. The covenant parties then passed between the halves indicating they were irrevocably bound together in blood.

Does this seem unnecessarily gruesome? Why would God demand the lives of animals just to seal a promise? I believe the answer is this: When God gives his word, he essentially gives life, whereas people are somewhat careless with their words. We throw them around like extra air.

But God's words are his very essence, *"In the beginning was the word, and the word was with God, and the word was God."* (John1:1, NIV). The very universe we live in is held together, literally, by the word of our Lord Jesus. Withdraw the word, and everything collapses. In order to get humans to take his words seriously, God demonstrates their importance by equating them with life itself. He wasn't being grisly because he enjoyed it. He was giving Abram fair warning that when entering into a covenant with God, Abram was laying his very life on the line.

The cutting in halves of the sacrificial animals spoke of the end of existing lives for the sake of a new covenant. The sacred nature of this bod was attested to by the shedding of lifeblood.

A quick review shows three components to the covenant between Abram and God.

1) There had to be a sacrifice

2) There had to be the death of an existing independent life.

3) There had to be shed blood.

Let's place these three components in context of a marriage covenant by asking these questions. What happens to a marriage if there is no sacrifice? What happens to a marriage if there is not a death to existing independent lifestyles? And is there blood shed at the consummation of a marriage covenant?

Two of these questions are easy. One of the vows we made during our wedding ceremony goes something like this: "Forsaking all others, I vow to keep myself only unto you, as long as we both shall live." If that's not a sacrifice and the death of an independent lifestyle, I don't know what is.

But what about the shedding of blood? You may think this part faded away with time. But God didn't forget about this aspect of covenant. We all know that the marriage covenant is sealed by the sexual union. When the virgin couple marries, and has their first intimate sexual experience, the woman's hymen is broken, and blood is shed. The blood covenant entered into by the husband and the wife is symbolic of the covenant God establishes with his people through the shedding of Christ's blood.

Marriage is sacred. Try to think of something more sacred...you can't! Marriage is IT as far as earthly relationships go. It is meant to be a blood covenant, a sharing of lives. That's why God wants both the man and woman to be virgins when they marry.

So many marry after losing their virginity, and

I believe this breaks the heart of God. But it doesn't nullify the marriage covenant. We know that God won't restore the physical virginity to the individual, but he does have a way to spiritually restore their virginity. Through repentance and forgiveness, God will always restore us from all unrighteousness (see 1 John1:9)

Understanding the serious "blood" nature of the covenant helps us to grab hold of God's perspective. Everything he does is designed to bring us closer to him. When a husband and wife live according to their marriage vows, all the power of a covenant keeping God is behind them and their marriage. God's power and authority stand against every enemy that would threaten it from without or within. Keeping a covenant with God and each other is the greatest force the world has ever known because it binds us together with love—and the Bible is clear that love is an undefeatable power.

But God has also said he will send a curse on our lives if we mistreat the institution of marriage. In the book of Malachi, God gives us two reasons why he would not be pleased with a marriage covenant.

1) We become un-equally yoked by marrying a non-believer.

2) We divorce the wife of our youth.

(Malachi 2:1-2, NIV) says *'And now, o ye priests, this commandment is for you. If you do not listen, and if you do not set your heart to honor my name,' says the Lord Almighty, 'I will send a curse upon you, and I will curse your blessings. Yes, I have already cursed them, because you have not set you heart to honor me'.*

(Malachi 2:10-12, NIV) says, *'Have we not all one father? Did not one God create us? Why do we profane the covenant of our fathers by breaking faith with one another? Judah has broken faith. A detestable thing has been committed in Israel and in Jerusalem: Judah has profaned the Lord's holy institution which he loves, by marrying the daughter of a foreign God. As for the man who does this, being awake and aware, may the Lord cut him off from the tents of Jacob—even though he brings offerings to the Lord Almighty'.*

Malachi tells us that we profane the holy institution of marriage by marrying a non-believer. He is not talking about non-believers marrying non-believers, but Christians who know what they are doing. Why does God hate this? Because non-believers tend to turn believers hearts away from God. (What is a Christian to do if they have already married a non-believer? The scriptures teach that you are to stay with them (1 Cor. 7:10-13), indicating again just how much God hates divorce.)

The second reason God will allow a curse to come onto those who break a blood covenant mentioned in Malachi reads like this:

'Another thing you do: you flood the Lord's alter with tears. You weep and wail because he no longer pays attention to your offerings or accepts them with pleasure from your hands. You ask, Why?' It is because the Lord is acting as the witness between you and the wife of your youth, because you have broken faith with her, though she is your partner, the wife of your marriage covenant. Has he not made them one? In flesh and spirit they are His. And why one? Because he was seeking Godly offspring. So guard yourself in your spirit, and do not break faith with the wife of your youth. 'I hate divorce,' says the Lord God of Israel, 'and I hate a man's covering himself with violence as well as with his garment,' says the Lord Almighty. So guard yourself in your spirit, and do not break faith. (Malachi 2:13-16, NIV)

I understand that in the dispensation of grace we live under today, Jesus became the curse for the payment of our sin. (Galatians 3:13, NIV) says, Jesus willingly became the curse for us by hanging on the tree. (cross). But anytime we willingly go against God's divine order, and break the covenant that has been sealed in blood, there will always be residual consequences for our actions— even though we have been saved from death, which is the ultimate result of sin.

In divorce, the consequences of the curse are obvious and diverse. The curse is revealed in the lives of our children, and the damaged personalities they bring into adulthood. I was recently speaking to one of my adult daughters about Christmas when I noticed tears in her eyes. I asked her " what is wrong honey?" and her response was, "Dad it was not supposed to be this way, I should not have to decide who's house I will be at on Christmas, yours or moms." The only response I had at that moment was, "I am sorry that I have put our family through this." Divorce's painful effects are lifelong and unending. The curse is revealed in our immediate family and our friends, and the wounds we inflict on them as a result. It is revealed in our finances, which are almost always shattered. It is revealed in the cruel injustice, the oppression, the violent dealings with one another, and the damage we cause to our spouse's life. What Malachi prophesied thousands of years ago is lived out in the homes of broken families everywhere today. The choice is still the same: you can choose the covenant or the curse. Tragically, millions have chosen the curse.

CHAPTER THREE

"FOR BETTER OR WORSE..."

I heard of a man who returned to the pastor that had performed his marriage ceremony and began to lay out all the complaints that he had against his wife, saying she was cold, grouchy, uncooperative, and a tightwad. Finally, the pastor interrupted him and said, "Now John, do you remember that you took her for better or for worse?" He replied, "Yeah, but she's much worse than I took her for."

God set a standard for marriage, and recorded it in Scripture. Simply put, it was "for better or worse."

A few years ago I had a dream, and in that dream was a plumb bob. This was strange because

I couldn't remember ever using a plumb bob. When I woke up I went to the Scriptures to see if the Lord was trying to tell me something, and sure enough, in the book of Amos, The Lord had shown Amos a plumb bob as well. (Amos 7:7-9, NIV) reads: *This is what he showed me: The Lord was standing by a wall that had been built true to plumb, with a plumb line in his hand. And the Lord asked me, 'What do you see, Amos?' 'A plumb line,' I replied. Then the Lord said, 'Look, I am setting a plumb line among my people Israel; I will spare them no longer.'*

In short, God told Amos, "I'm setting a standard for Israel. A standard that will enable them to measure an absolute truth."

In America, nobody seems to own plumb bobs anymore. You can't find them in garages, tool shops, on television, in the newspaper, in many churches...I'm not talking about the tool, but about the moral standard. Americans live in a society that believes in no absolute truth. Many feel that everything is relative, that there is no yardstick or plumb bob to measure by.

But we still have an absolute truth, and it's called the Word of God. Unfortunately, most people in this country ignore or despise the Word and its teachings, which mean the cultural landscape looks quite a bit different than God wants it to.

What does that have to do with divorce? Let me ask you this: Can you think of a more common cultural feature than the casual way we treat separation and divorce? If we are going to discuss ways to prevent divorce, we must look at it as reality. Divorce has reached epidemic proportions, and the church that Jesus died for has not been immune from this disease.

A recent survey indicates that if the divorce rate continues as it has in the past, it's possible that 70 percent of our society will be victims of divorce. Single-parent homes and blended families are everywhere around us. Don't be deceived by the seemingly drop in the American divorce rate. This is only because more couples are now living with one another rather than getting married, so when they break up, naturally it is not counted as divorce. Even though children may now be involved.

We have become numb not plumb.

Let's shake off our own cultural dust for a moment and take a journey back to Judea, to listen in on a conversation that Jesus was having with some Pharisees on this same topic. (Matthew 19:1, KJV) says, *And it came to pass, that when Jesus had finished these sayings, he departed from Galilee, and came into the coasts of Judea beyond* the Jordan.

It's important to note here that the "sayings that Jesus had just finished" were about forgiveness. Jesus taught how the "torturers" were enabled to come and take their toll on the bodies, and minds and emotions of those who had chosen not to forgive (a chilling thought!).

This is relevant to us because these same areas are affected I divorce. Remember this: Where true forgiveness is present, hardness of heart is destroyed.

Jesus followed his teaching on forgiveness with teaching on marriage and divorce. This was not a coincidence—forgiveness is essential to preventing divorce. It goes on: (Matthew 19:2-9, NIV) *And a great multitude followed him; and he healed them there. Some Pharisees came to him to test him. They asked, 'Is it lawful for a man to divorce his wife for any and every reason?' 'Haven't you read,' he replied, 'that at the beginning the Creator made them male and female, and said, for this cause shall a man leave his father and mother, and shall cleave to his wife; and the two shall become one flesh? So they are no longer two, but one. Therefore what God has joined together, let man not separate.'*

'Why then,' they asked, 'did Moses command that a man give his wife a certificate of divorce

and send her away?' Jesus replied, 'Moses permitted you to divorce your wives because your hearts were hard. But it was not this way from the beginning. I tell you that anyone who divorces his wife, except for marital unfaithfulness, and marries another woman commits adultery.'

The conversation between Jesus and these Pharisees stemmed from an age-old debate concerning when it was okay for a man to divorce his wife.

During Old Testament times women were given a pretty raw deal. When a woman was married, she married knowing that she could never divorce her husband. But her husband could divorce her at any time, for any reason. Sound unfair? It was! If a man found any displeasure in his wife, she could be booted from her very home.

There were two schools of thought in Jesus' day on divorce. The conservative rabbis were of the school of Shammai. They held that divorce could only be granted due to unfaithfulness in the marriage covenant.

The liberal rabbis were of the school of Hellel. Their view on divorce was "a man could divorce his wife for any and every reason." Their theology came from (Deuteronomy 24:1, KJV) which reads: *When a man hath taken a wife, and married her, and it comes to pass that she find no favor in his eyes, because he hath found some uncleanness in her: then let him write her a bill of divorcement, and hive it in her hand, and send her out of his house.*

In other words, if your wife burnt the bread, you had grounds for divorce; if she accidentally put an extra crease in your shirt while ironing it, *"and she found no favor"* in your eyes, she was finished. The man's only obligation was to provide for her financially until she died. Note that many of these divorced wives met very early deaths.

The atmosphere was tense between Jesus and the Pharisees who were always on his case. You can imagine the crackle of a good debate. The Pharisees in this passage in Matthew were not trying to resolve this issue of divorce,
they were trying to trap Jesus by getting him to choose a side. But they were dealing with a new kind of man, because Jesus never chooses sides. He chooses truth. Rather than deal with the issue of divorce, Jesus dealt with the standard of marriage. *And he answered and said unto them, 'Have ye not read, that he which made them at the beginning made them male and female?'* (Matthew 19:4, KJV).

Jesus said God made us male and female, two halves that complement one another. The Scripture teaches us that Eve was to Adam his "completeness." They complemented one another. Jesus continued in (Matthew 19:5, KJV) and said, *'For this cause shall a man leave his father and mother, and shall cleave to his wife: and the two shall be one flesh.'* This word "cleave" means to "join oneself to," "to adhere to," "to be glued to."

God's will and his purpose in marriage was that a couple be glued to one another, emotionally, physically, and spiritually, to the degree that they operated as one single unit. The two were never to be two again, but one with each other for life. That was God's standard—his plumb bob—for marriage.

This "oneness" is displayed in the blood covenant that we saw earlier. When blood is shed there is a real or symbolic death of one life so that a new life ("covenant") can spring up. God no more wants people in a marriage covenant to separate and become two again than he wanted the animal halves to walk down the mountain and rejoin again, nullifying his covenant with Abram.

God is a god of commitment. Once he makes a promise, he keeps it—and he wants us to do the same, even in the face of great adversity and death. We could spend a good deal of time talking about the grounds for divorce, and the discussion would never end. But we could not, with all our words, get past one simple fact: God hates divorce, and God condemns divorce.

But even though divorced people will bear the effects of divorce's curse, God remains merciful, and will never condemn divorced people. God will never condemn or accuse people whatsoever (see John 3:17). It is his nature to judge rightly and love greatly. Praise the Lord that he loves us! But it is not his nature to accuse. God has given us a standard for marriage for our own good, but a discussion of divorce would not be complete without a discussion of God's mercy.

The truth is, no matter what heinous sin we commit, either knowingly or unknowingly, God will be at the other side to receive us if we ask for forgiveness. Murder, rape, theft and even divorce—God's mercy surpasses them all.

Does this mean that, as a believer, I have the license to sin? Absolutely not. No man is going to make a mockery of God. Does it mean that god will condone my divorce if I think I have good reasons? No. God will not condone divorce.

Jesus said divorce was granted in Moses' day due to the hardness of man's heart. The certificate of divorce was given because of God's mercy, not his will.

It's his will that this husband and wife walk in the unity and oneness that was set in motion the moment the covenant was consummated. God's standard is one man with one woman— for life. In Moses' day, the hardness of heart had accelerated over the generations until God gave them a way out. The same thing happens today as we become immune to breaking God's law.

For those of you in a situation where divorce has been considered, I challenge you with this statement: Whatever is condoned by this generation, will be practiced by the next generation.

In a family where divorce has been condoned in the previous generation, divorce will be practiced in the generation that follows. If you don't believe me, simply ask divorced people if their parents got divorced?

If divorce has already been a factor in your family, like it has in mine, don't hide the devastation from your children. This is an area in life that I do not want my children to follow me in. I tell them how divorce has not only affected me emotionally, but others as well. Tell them how divorce will devastate them financially, and don't leave out the fact that divorce will devastate them spiritually. No one is immune.

Our children see mommy and daddy divorce. From all appearances it may seem that mommy and daddy made it through; therefore divorce must be acceptable and okay. What many children fail to see is that in the aftermath of divorce, mommy and daddy are dying inside themselves.

In a magazine I recently read on an airplane, an article listed the things that cause the greatest amount of stress and pain. The article listed, in sequence:

2) The death of a spouse.

3) The death of a child.

4) The death of a sibling.

5) The loss of a body part.

6) Becoming handicapped.

The list continued all the way down to "bankruptcy." But did you notice that I omitted number one? At the very top of the list, more painful than anything else, was:

1) Divorce.

And this was a secular publication! Where there is the death of a spouse, or the loss of a body part, God uses time as the source of grief, to heal the memory. But with divorce, it's ever present.

As one of the men I interviewed said, "You live divorce; it's a lifestyle." Notice that the people who speak out the loudest against divorce are divorced people. We would do well to listen to the voice of experience, even if our society still refuses to use God's plumb bob.

CHAPTER FOUR

"FOR RICHER OR POORER..."

Getting richer financially does not guarantee success in a marriage. In most cases, the opposite is true: wealth is more difficult to handle than poverty. An old saying goes, "If 99 men out of 100 can handle poverty, only one can handle wealth."

This may surprise you, but of all the divorced couples I have interviewed, none have told me they divorced because they were poor. Finances can add pressure to a marriage that is already experiencing difficulties, but it is rarely the root cause. Many blame finances when the real reason is unremitting selfishness being displayed in their spending patterns. That's not a financial problem, my friend—it's a heart problem.

Besides, if being poor financially always leads to divorce, my parents would have never celebrated nearly 70 years of marriage. And if people want to compare "poor stories" I can stay up with the best of them. As a child, we lived on a diet of black-eyed peas for more than a month, simply because there was nothing else to eat. (To this day I don't like black-eyed peas.) I can remember living for three months in a metro truck on a canal bank in Mendota, California, because our family didn't have a home. As the youngest of five children, I thought we were just camping. Now I have five children of my own—I can only imagine the pressure this must have put on my mother and father's marriage. But somehow, they made it.

That "somehow" is a missing component in many of today's marriages. That "somehow" is called "commitment," and that commitment comes to bear on our finances. God has set things up so that personal commitments are rewarded with financial blessings. The opposite is also true: The breaking of personal commitments is cursed with financial ruin. Every individual I interviewed has told me that in the aftermath of divorce they were financially devastated. I can now attest that to be true in my own life. Ten years after the divorce was final, I am still dealing with the financial pitfalls divorce brings with it. No one is immune. One of the stories I was told still sticks in my mind.

We'll call him Mike. Mike was divorced, and he told me what happened after his decision:

"Divorce financially destroyed my life. It put my children in poverty. I had to go on welfare while my children were in school because I couldn't afford child care while I worked. I had never been on welfare before. It had never been an option before the divorce, your children no longer belong to you. Now they were owned by the court system and the county I lived in. Anything I wanted to do where my children were concerned had to be cleared by the court system and the county. It's like living in a fishbowl with the court system always observing your movement. The freedom you once had with your family is now gone.

There are no rules in divorce and it seems the games never stop. My advice to anyone who is considering divorce is this: Don't do it! Get counseling, get help, do whatever you must do to save your family. Even though this seems as if it is the most devastating time in your life, with divorce as an added ingredient, it only gets worse."

Is there a reason why financial devastation

and divorce go hand in hand? I believe it's tied directly to the curse that Malachi prophesied would take place on those who break the marriage covenant and divorce.

"And now, you priests, this warning is for you. If you do not listen, and if you do not resolve to honor my name," says the Lord Almighty, "I will send a curse on you, and I will curse your blessings. Yes, I have already cursed them, because you have not resolved to honor me.

"Because of you I will rebuke your descendants; I will smear on your faces the dung from your festival sacrifices, and you will be carried off with it." (Malachi 2:1-3, NIV).

Divorce bankrupts people emotionally, physically, spiritually, and financially. When Malachi said that God would curse our blessings, that is what he meant. Do we think that God's promises end? Surely not. He is from everlasting to everlasting. If He said he would curse our blessings, we should expect Him to do it; otherwise, He would be pretty unreliable.

The word "blessing" in the Hebrew means things that cause us to prosper financially. When we covenant with God to stay with our spouse "for richer or for poorer," He takes that seriously. He also promises us that when we live by the standards He lays out for us, then every provision that we need will be met by Him.

God gave men—as in males—an order of sequence to life in the Book of Genesis. Toward the end of the sixth day of creation, God created man. *And God said, 'Let us make man in our image, after our likeness: and let them have dominion over the fish of the sea, and over the fowl of the air, and over the cattle, and over all the earth, and over every creeping thing that creepeth upon the earth.' So God created man in his own image, in the image of God created He him; male and female created He them* (Genesis 1:26, 27, KJV).

It seems that God created man and then in verse 27 He immediately created woman. But that's not really the case. In between verses 26 and 27, we can place nearly everything that happened in the entire second chapter of Genesis. You see, before God ever gave Adam a wife, He gave him a job. *And the Lord God took the man, and put him into the Garden of Eden to dress it and to keep it* (Genesis 2:15, KJV).

God gave Adam a mission and a challenge. So the first principle we find for marriage and family is for men: Before God provides you with a wife, He expects you to have a job. No job, no wife!

The job God gave Adam is important to how man and woman relate. *Now the Lord God had formed out of the ground all the beasts of the field and all the birds of the air. He brought them to the man to see what he would name them; and whatever the man called each living creature, that was its name. So the man gave names to all the livestock, the birds of the air and all the beasts of the field. But for Adam no suitable helper was found* (Genesis 2:19, 20, NIV).

Adam was given a very large responsibility—to name every animal in the world. Wouldn't you say that this job added to Adam's character? It made Adam feel competent. God told Adam to name all the animals, to dress and tend to the Garden, and in so doing, gave Adam a sense of value. God had even placed in Adam the ability to confer value on things. This job gave Adam a sense of power and achievement. He suddenly became results-oriented. He began to feel competent at his job.

All men want to feel competent in what they do, and the biblical basis for this is clear. Adam's self-image related to the task for which God created him. He was a provider for those animals, a nurturer to that wonderful Garden. Now he was ready to become a husband in the full sense of the word.

The word "husband" in the Hebrew language is translated "husbandman," meaning "nurturer" or "farmer." God has given men the responsibility to tend to "the farm"—their job. But "the farm" also consists of our family members. Adam himself sensed the incompleteness in his self, and having performed well at his job, God was ready to entrust him with the full responsibility of a man: to take care not just of animals and plants, but other human beings.

It was an awesome responsibility. *So the Lord God caused the man to fall into a deep sleep; and while he was sleeping, he took one of the man's ribs and closed up the place with flesh. Then the Lord God made a woman from the rib he had taken out of the man, and he brought her to the man. The man said, 'This is now bone of my bones and flesh of my flesh; she shall be called woman, for she was taken out of man'* (Genesis 2:21-23, NIV).

Little did Adam know that his world was about to change drastically. I imagine his first reaction upon waking up and squinting at this being beside him was. "Whoa, thank you God, you outdid yourself this time!" With the arrival of woman, the nature of Adam's job deepened considerably.

The first relationship he'd had was with his job. He had complete control. He could boss those animals around and they would obey every word, because they had been created to do so. But this wasn't going to fly with Eve, because she was a person, like himself. Now Adam was going to have to learn a new kind of responsibility with her.

To further frustrate things, Eve was in many ways different from Adam. Her first relationship wasn't with a job, but with a person: Adam. That tells us that women were created to be more personal, and to take things more personally. (How many men have received that revelation at some point on life's journey?) Is it any wonder why men tend to think of their identities in terms of occupation, while women get their identities from their relationships and the home?

When God created the man to be provider, that meant more than just finances. Men are to provide stability and security in the home. They are to be the provider of love for wives and children.

Contrary to what our society tries to dictate to us, God has placed the man in the home to be the primary provider for families financially. God has placed women in the home to be the primary homemaker. That is God's order and design. Does that mean that men should never help with housework? Absolutely not. Does that mean that women should never work outside the home? Absolutely not. It simply means that God has given a standard for us to live by and follow, and when we follow it, it works.

Let's take the idea of man as the "husband" of the house beyond the financial realm and round out our understanding of this aspect of marriage. We have seen the financial consequences of divorce. But what about spiritually?

The "provider standard" that God has laid down in the home is violated when divorce occurs, as the male is normally removed from the provisional position that God placed him in, and the woman is thrust into the position of provider, where biblically she was never designed to be.

Any reversal of a principle God lays down will meet disaster. It's a natural consequence. Paul in his letter to Titus reminds us of this principle: *You must teach what is in accord with sound doctrine. Teach the older men to be temperate, worthy of respect, self-controlled, and sound in faith, in love and endurance. Likewise, teach the older women to be reverent in the way they live, not to be slanderers or addicted to much wine, but to teach what is good. Then they can train the younger women to love their husbands and children, to be self-controlled and pure, to be busy at home, to be kind, and to be subject to their husbands, so that no one will malign the word of God. Similarly, encourage the young men to be self-controlled. In everything set them an example by doing what is good. In your teaching show integrity, seriousness and soundness of speech that cannot be condemned, so that those who oppose you may be ashamed because they have nothing bad to say about us.* (Titus 2:1-8, NIV)

If someone came into your home, what kind of environment would they find? Would your enemies (if you have any) be ashamed to say anything bad about you? Anytime we find the type of home described in Titus, we find God's principle being lived out—and Paul says God's principle is inviolable and impervious to criticism.

The male provides security, stability, love, and respect in the home. The female submits feely to her husband, willingly praises him for the treatment she is receiving, and has a great sense of security. God's picture of a home is truly a beautiful thing; liberating, not oppressive.

When the provider principle is abdicated to the enemy, we lose out both financially and spiritually. We have already lost a generation of young people because we have lost a generation of parents. We've essentially told our children to raise themselves. We've abdicated responsibility of the home to the television set, to video games, to the day care center; to the church, when by all rights the responsibility of the home starts with the parents. Abdicating the provider principle sets the curse in motion. The vow was for richer or for poorer.

Victims of divorce will be the first to tell you that "being richer" will never provide happiness in a family. It's only found in a personal relationship with Jesus Christ. If finances have been a factor in the downfall of your marriage, and you can't seem to get them under control, I recommend a book to you and your spouse. It is entitled *Marriage Savers,* by Michael J. McManus (Zondervan Press). I will end this critical chapter by quoting from page 163 of McManus's book:

The Ten Commandments of financial management.

1. Acknowledge biblical principles of money management. God owns it all (Ps. 24:1). Faith requires action (Matt. 25:14-30).
2. Establish priorities. Our tithe (Prov. 3:9-10). Our taxes (Luke 20:25). Our savings (Prov.23:20). Our families (1 Tim. 5:8). Our giving (Prov. 11:24-25).
3. Know your basic money personality type. Are you a hoarder, spender, money monk, money avoider, money worrier, money amasser, risk taker, or risk avoider?
4. Establish goals—giving, saving, standard of living, children's education, financial independence, retirement-and put these goals in dollar terms, then set a timetable to

accomplish them.

5. Know your financial position—what you own and what you owe; what your earn and what you spend (Prov. 27:24).
6. Control you spending. Budget wisely, avoid debt (Prov. 24:3-4).
7. Protect yourself against all insurable risks. Do not risk what you can't afford to lose.
8. Get good advice and shop around (Prov. 15:22, 23:23).
9. Be alert and patient (Prov. 21:5).
10. Count on God's faithfulness, direction and love (Isaiah. 46:3-4).

CHAPTER FIVE

"IN SICKNESS AND IN HEALTH..."

Admit it. The thought probably crossed all of our minds during the wedding ceremony, as the pastor droned on. "What happens if this person I'm about to marry becomes ill? What happens if he or she comes to the place in their life where he or she can no longer function in the capacity that they function today?" With a shudder and a shake of the head, such thoughts can be pushed back and lost in a sea of romanticism...for a while.

Each person entering the marriage covenant must come to the conclusion that they will stick by their bride or groom even in the darkest of days. This includes debilitating diseases, incurable cancers, automobile accidents—you name it. It may seem like a scary proposition at first. But what's even scarier is what happens to your health when you divorce.

In Marriage Savers, Michael McManus writes this: "Divorce has become so commonplace in the United States that many assume that its pain and consequences are limited to anguish. Not so says Dr. David Larson, president of the National Institute of HealthCare research. Divorce is a hazard to your health. 'Research studies show that divorce and the process of marital breakup puts people at much higher risk for the psychiatric and physical disease…even cancer.

Being divorced and a nonsmoker is only slightly less dangerous than smoking a pack or more of cigarettes a day and staying married. Every type of terminal cancer strikes divorced individuals of either sex, more frequently than it does married people.

Research reveals that divorced men are twice as likely to die from heart disease, stroke, hypertension, and cancer as married men in any given year. Death for the divorced is four times more likely via auto accident and suicide; seven times higher by cirrhosis of the liver and pneumonia; and eight times greater by murder. Divorced people are ten times more likely to suffer psychiatric illness.'

Dr. Larson's study researched 20,000 women between the ages of 18 and 55, and found that married women are far less prone to physical illness than are single women who suffer more chronic conditions than that of married women.

For example, divorced women's odds of dying in a given year from cancer of the mouth, digestive organs, lungs and breasts, are two to three times that of married women. Dr. Larson's conclusion is this: He rejects the idea that divorce is an answer to marital problems. It's wiser to improve a marriage rather than dissolve it, and physicians should encourage marital therapy for troubled marriages." (pp. 32-33)

In terms of physical health, divorce is a radical step in the wrong direction. No amount of post marital counseling is going to relieve the stress that the mind and body naturally feel when they are torn from their life mate.

Just as bad as physical sickness in a marriage is the relational sickness. What happens to a marriage that neglects the health of the union? Or the communication of the union? Or what happens if the male fails to take the role of spiritual leader? The union becomes sick.

The dictionary defines "sickness" as "an abnormal unhealthy condition, a state of being thoroughly tired; weary." This defines many marriages in our society today. "Abnormal...unhealthy...thoroughly tired...weary."

If we neglect the health of our bodies, our bodies will die at an accelerated speed. If we neglect the health of our spiritual life, spiritually we die. And if we neglect the health of our marriage, our marriage has no other choice but death. Why would we think otherwise?

(Proverbs 14:12, ASV) says: *There is a way which seems right unto a man; but the end thereof are the ways of death.* Divorce is like a death without a funeral. There is no closure, no end. It's an open casket that is ever before you, never coming to final resting place.

The apostle Paul told the Corinthian church, (1 Cor. 7:10, 11, NIV) *A wife is not to depart from her husband... And a husband is not to divorce his wife.* Paul told us this because he knew the seriousness of the covenant.

God desires to breathe fresh life into any marriage that has become sick. Look at His promise: (Prov. 14:32, NIV) *When calamity comes, the wicked are brought down, but even in death the righteous have a refuge.* Even when your marriage seems like it dead, with Christ we have a refuge, and hope.

Jesus was invited to a wedding. (John 2:1-11,

NIV and ASV) *On the third day a wedding took place at Cana in Galilee. Jesus' mother was there, and Jesus and his disciples had also been invited to the wedding. When the wine was gone, Jesus' mother said to him, 'They have no more wine.'*

'Dear woman, why do you involve me?' Jesus replied. 'My time has not yet come.' His mother said to the servants, 'Whatever he says to you, do it.' Nearby stood six stone water jars, the kind used by the Jews for ceremonial washing, each holding from twenty to thirty gallons.

Jesus said to the servants,   'Fill the jars with water'; so they filled them to the brim. Then he told them, 'Now draw some out and take it to the master of the banquet.' They did so, and the master of the banquet tasted the water that had been turned into wine.

He did not realize where it had come from, though the servants who had drawn the water knew. Then he called the bridegroom aside and said, 'Everyone brings out the choice wine first and then the cheaper wine after the guests have had too much to drink; but you have saved the best till now.'

This beginning of his signs did Jesus in Cana of Galilee, and manifested his glory; and his disciples believed on him.

What would it have been like to have Jesus,

the savior of the world, show up at *your* wedding?

As the pastor of Family Strong, the marriage and family ministry at our church in Modesto, California, I have the privilege of performing many wedding ceremonies.

Recently, I was performing one of these weddings and the thought came to me as the bride was walking down the aisle. "What difference would it have made in this wedding if Jesus were seated on the front row? How would the family's preparation have changed? What difference would He have made in the atmosphere of the rehearsal and reception?"

John doesn't provide many details about this wedding. We don't even know the names of the bride and groom that stood there that day 2,000 years ago. But one thing we can be sure of: The presence of Jesus Christ at this young couple's wedding had to make an impression on them that lasted the rest of their lives. We know this because when Jesus Christ is the invited guest in our marriage, he still performs such miracles— including healing "sick" relationships.

The first thing we should do, no matter how long we have been married, or how healthy we think our marriage is, is to re-invite Jesus to be our guest of honor. Jesus must be the foundation that we build our families upon. Without His foundation, the structure is sure to fall.

Dr. Tony Evans, the great preacher from Dallas, Texas, told a story about having his house painted. When the painter began painting, the first thing he did was put putty in a large crack in the corner of one of the rooms. The painting job was complete and looked wonderful. But after a few weeks Dr. Evans noticed the crack had re-appeared. He called the painter back.

The painter was glad to re-repair the crack and re-painted the entire area. Dr. Evans was happy and satisfied. A few more weeks passed and lo and behold, the crack was back. This time Dr. Evans was a little more upset, he quickly called the painter to return to his home at once. When the painter arrived, he once again looked at the crack and told Dr. Evans, "I can come back every month to repair and repaint this crack, but it will never really be repaired because the problem is not your wall, your problem Dr. Evans, is your foundation. The foundation of your home is evidently built on shifting sand, so quit wasting your money on paint, and repair your foundation."

That story is true of many marriages. We have some serious cracks in our relationships and all we do is paint over them. When in reality we need to repair our foundations. Let me ask you this today,

"What is the foundation that your marriage is built on?" If you want your house to stand, let Jesus be your foundation. Re-invite Him into your marriage, not as a guest, but as the Master.

The second principal we can learn from the story of Jesus's first miracle is this: Do whatever He tells you to do, no matter how crazy it might seem! Who would have ever thought that pouring plain water into some old ceremonial cleansing pots would produce the freshest wine they ever tasted? Jesus has new wine for your marriage. He always saves the best for the last.

(Eccles. 7:8, NIV) *The end of a matter is better than its beginning, and patience is better than pride.*

I close this chapter with two things. First is an excerpt from an article in USA Today called "World War Two's Unbreakable Bonds: Five couples celebrate 50 years of marriage. How did they do it?" After that I list ten steps for those who have "sick" relationships.

"When we were married, the word divorce was not even said,' says Norma Neufeld, 68 of Deerfield Beach, Fl., who will celebrate her fiftieth wedding anniversary this spring with her husband, Milton.

'Those who were divorced were not actually shunned, but they would say things like, "Oh, she's divorced!" It was noted.'

Neufeld said couples married in the 1940's and stayed together for any number of reasons. If it wasn't religion telling them not to part, it was society. Or they stayed for the children. It was not until the 1960's that divorce began to lose its stigma, and by then these couples had been married almost 20 years.

Compromise and forgiveness are often cited as the keys to success, although one man summed up the ingredients of a successful marriage in two words: "Yes dear." ...It seems there is a thread that runs through all successful marriages. Respect, listening to the other person, and letting that person be who they really are. It all sounds so simple, but isn't that what we all want? We all want love, respect, and kindness."

Here are ten steps to help bring health to an otherwise unhealthy marriage:

1) Set a time and place for discussion.

2) Define the problem or issue of disagreement.

3) Define how you each contribute to the

problem.

4) List all things you have done that have not been successful solving the problem.

5) Brainstorm and list all possible solutions.

6) Discuss each of these solutions.

7) Agree on one solution to try.

8) Agree how each person will work toward the solution.

9) Set a time for another meeting to review your progress.

10) Reward each other as you contribute to the solution.

CHAPTER SIX

"TO LOVE AND TO HONOR..."

To love and to honor is not a difficult thing to do as the onset of our relationship. But an untended marriage quickly becomes like an untended garden—overcome with weeds of controversy, eaten up by insects of lost intimacy, and destroyed by the devastation of dishonoring words and deeds that seem to flow so freely.

One of the most powerful statements in all the Bible for husbands is found in first Peter:
(1 Peter 3:7, ASV), *"You husbands, in like manner, dwell with your wives according to knowledge, giving honor unto the woman, as unto the weaker vessel, as being also joint-heirs of the grace of life;*

to the end that your prayers may not be hindered".

When Peter refers to the wife as *"the weaker vessel"*, he is not talking about the husband being able to out arm wrestle his wife, because he is stronger. What this verse actually means is that a husband is to view his wife as a 'priceless creation', as an "irreplaceable piece of fine art", more valued than precious gold, and to honor her is such a way.

Men, do you want your prayers to be hindered? Fight with your wife. Leave conflicts unresolved. Burn with anger against her—then see how far you get with God!

To the wife the Bible speaks this: (1 Peter 3:1, 2, NIV). *"Wives, in the same way be submissive to your husbands so that, if any of them do not believe the word, they may be won over without words by the behavior of their wives, when they see the purity and reverence of your lives."*

The most effective way to open the door to needed changes in your relationship is to honor your spouse. Once we have decided to honor, love is and action we will give no matter how we feel. Genuine love is honor put into action, regardless of the cost. The vow that we made to one another on our wedding day was to love and to honor. Without one, the other is impossible.

Without a doubt, the concept of honor is the single most important principal I know of for building healthy marriages. Honor is not only the basis for our earthly relationships, it's also at the heart of our relationship with God. (Matt. 6:19-21, NIV), *"Do not store up for yourselves treasures on earth, where moth and rust destroy, and where thieves break in and steal. But store up for yourselves treasures in heaven, where moth and rust do not destroy, and where thieves do not break in and steal. For where your treasure is, there your heart will be also."*

For anyone contemplating divorce, the first question we need to consider is this: "Where is your treasure?" Jesus said *"where your treasure is there your heart will be also."* If there was ever a time when your source of treasure was found in your spouse, then it is possible for the treasure to be discovered once again. So often we hear people say "I just don't love you anymore." I can tell you now, that love is a decision. We decide who or what we are going to love by deciding who or what we are going to honor. We honor what we place value on.

I used to think the opposite of *honor* was *dishonor*, but now that I have experienced divorce myself, and interviewed many other victims of divorce, I no longer believe that. Now I believe the opposite of honor is *SELFISHNESS*. Dishonor is a by-product of selfishness. There seems to be a prevailing spirit of selfishness that hovers over every couple in the process of divorce.

Following are some quotes from the interviews I have conducted with divorced people. "I learned to be a great manipulator, simply because I desired to control every portion of her life." "None of my needs were being met." "I didn't want to come home, cook dinner, or sleep with him any longer, because my needs were now being met by another man." " I didn't care anymore what anyone else thought or said, I've lived to please others my entire life, now I am going to please myself."

One lady summed it up very nicely in a moment of blinding clarity: "Now I know I was being very selfish. When I had the children, the selfishness should have stopped. Now I've come to realize that contentment can only be found in a relationship with the Lord. If anyone divorces for selfish reasons, they will live with the consequences for the rest of their lives."

The Apostle Paul wrote in (Romans 12:10, NIV), *"Be devoted to one another in brotherly love. Honor one another above yourselves."* During biblical times, The word "honor" carried a meaning that has been all but lost by translation and time. For a Greek person living in Christ's day, "honor" called to mind something "heavy or weighty." Gold, for example, was the perfect picture of honor because it was heavy and valuable at the same time. For the same Greek person, the word "dishonor" actually meant "mist: or "steam." Why? Because the lightest, most insignificant thing the Greeks could think of was steam rising off of a pot of boiling water. It was without any value.

Anytime we honor our spouse, we are actually telling him or her that who they are as a person, and what they say carries great weight with us. They are not just a "mist" in our lives. Just the opposite is true when we dishonor them.

When the prophet Malachi began to deal with the priests (the men) on the issue of divorce, note the reason they brought a curse upon themselves: (Malachi 2:14, NIV), "You ask, 'Why?' It is because the Lord is acting as the witness between you and the wife of your youth, because you have dealt treacherously with her, though she is your partner, the wife of your marriage covenant."

This word "treacherous" actually meant to deal deceitfully with, to be cruel to, and to dishonor. When God commands the husband of a marriage covenant to love his wife as Christ loved the church, he meant just that!

Jesus is our example of honor. Even when He was angry with people, He never dishonored one single human being. He may have condemned their actions, but He never dishonored them as a person.

The Apostle Paul tells us in (Ephesians 4:29 KJV), *"Let no corrupt communication proceed out of your mouth, but that which is good to the use of edifying, that it may minister grace unto the hearers."* Now, ask yourself this question: "Are the words I use when talking with my spouse ministering grace that honors him or her? Or are my words corrupt, conveying dishonor?" Don't be surprised if your answer makes you squirm. You are not alone my friend.

How do we change and bring honor into our marriage? Repent for your selfish attitudes! Understand that the first step toward honoring our spouse begins with honoring God. We honor God by spending time with Him in the Word, in prayer, and sharing our faith with others. The Bible says *"the fear of the Lord is the beginning of wisdom."* The word "fear" does not mean to be afraid of God. The word "fear" is translated "respect or honor." Honor God, then try honoring your spouse. It will be much easier.

The late Gary Smalley, who was a champion for marriages, in his book "Love is a Decision"

(Word Publishers) teaches the "a-h-h-h-h-h-h" principal. We can illustrate the principal this way. What do you think Peter's reaction was that day on the boat in the middle of a raging storm when they woke Jesus up?

(Mark 4:37-41, NIV) *A furious squall came up, and the waves broke over the boat, so that it was nearly swamped. 38 Jesus was in the stern, sleeping on a cushion. The disciples woke him and said to him, "Teacher, don't you care if we drown?" He got up, rebuked the wind and said to the waves, "Quiet! Be still!" Then the wind died down and it was completely calm. He said to his disciples, "Why are you so afraid? Do you still have no faith?" They were terrified and asked each other, "Who is this? Even the wind and the waves obey him!"* In other words: "AH-H-H-H-H-H-H!" A light had been turned on and they understood for a moment the *weight* of who Jesus was.

Think of Moses in front of the burning bush when the bush started talking to him. "AH-H-H-H-H-H! This is no ordinary bush." In the same way, honor is a reflex of the heart toward one who is deeply treasured. This life-changing attitude does not start with a feeling. It's a decision! The feeling of "awe" will follow.

Why is a dog considered man's best friend? Because you could be gone for two weeks on vacation or ten minutes to the mini-mart, and you dog will always greet you like his long lost buddy. Dogs naturally show honor. Why do men normally dislike cats? Because they don't give a rip how long you've been gone.

The "ah-h-h-h-h-h" principle can restore your marriage. It says to your spouse, "I can't believe I'm in the same room with you! My heart leaps just thinking about it." What you are actually saying is, "You're valuable to me." Ladies, take note: Men are extremely motivated by the "ah-h-h-h-h-h" principal. (Proverbs 15:30, KJV) says, *"The light of the eyes rejoices the heart: and a good report makes the bones fat."*

"AH-H-H-H-H-H" is in the eye of the beholder. When we honor someone, we make a decision that a person is special and important. Biblically, honor was not always something that had to be earned. It was given as an act of grace to someone who didn't deserve it. (Romans 5:8, NIV) *"But God demonstrates his own love for us in this: while we were still sinners, Christ died for us."* Just like Jesus, we sometimes need to honor someone apart from our feelings.

It's amazing how our attitude can change once we have decided that a certain individual is truly valuable. If you are struggling with this because you don't think your spouse deserves your honor, you need to ask yourself two questions: "Do I want my marriage to blossom or to wither?" and "What motivates me to honor someone?"

Marriages will not bloom without honor, and it is not really our choice whether or not we will honor our spouse, if we follow God's commands. If divorce has become an option for you, you need to honor your spouse not out of feelings but out of obedience to God's command that you do so.

Rest assured that when honor is in its right place, loving feelings will always follow. Jesus said, *"Where your treasure is there your heart will be as well."* When you decide that your spouse is a treasure, a warm, loving feeling will rise seemingly out of nowhere.

Ten dishonoring acts in the home:

1) Ignoring another person's opinion or advice.

2) Watching television while someone is trying to communicate with you.

3) Making jokes about another person's weak areas or shortcomings.

4) Verbal attacks or uncaring lectures.

5) Ignoring kind deeds done for you by others.

6) Distasteful habits practiced in front of family members.

7) Overcommitting ourselves to projects and neglecting our family.

8) Power struggles that leave one feeling dominated.

9) Treating in-laws as unimportant.

10) Unwillingness to admit when we are wrong and ask forgiveness.

Ten ways to honor your wife:

1) Take her out to eat when she is frustrated or tired.

2) If she is out for the evening, make sure she

doesn't come home to a messy house.

3) Make the bed in the morning.

4) Leave your "bad day" at work.

5) Talk with her until she is satisfied.

6) Don't offer solutions to complaints; she may just be venting; just listen.

7) Allow your wife to dream; don't be a "dream basher."

8) Let her have the remote control.

9) Kiss her hello and good-bye whenever you see her. You never know when it will be the last time you have that opportunity.

10) Wash her car.

CHAPTER SEVEN

"FORSAKING ALL OTHERS..." (PART 1)

I want to begin this chapter with a heart-breaking story which I call Romancing Regret. The woman's name is Lisa. I might add that all marital affairs end in heart-breaking stories. Should you choose to take this road that is well to traveled, you will not be immune from the destruction. Lisa's story is just one of many, of bad choices, leading to a fall.

"After 17 years of marriage I came to the end of my rope. My husband would never change, or so I thought. Something had to be done. So I decided to make a move—a move completely out of the house. At the time I convinced myself that it would be the best thing I had ever done. In reality, it turned out to be the worst mistake of my life.

When I moved out I did not foresee the great loneliness that was about to engulf me. I buried myself in my job, my hurt, and my anger.

Then another man entered my life. He renewed feelings in me that I thought were long lost. I loved receiving the flowers, being romanced, and appreciated as a woman. We spent hours on the phone and became emotionally attached. We both hurt, so we clung to each other.

That's when the sexual relationship began. I know now that the emotional affair began long before the physical. Having been raised in a Christian home, I knew this was wrong; however, I paid no heed to my conscience. I found great pleasure in his arms.

Then it ended. My life was a mess. The pain tortured me. It cut deep. The loneliness felt like a gaping chasm. I became even more vulnerable, and while attempting to recapture the good feelings, I walked straight into a second affair. Thinking I would find security, I was smacked right in the face by the falseness and cheapness of it.

The shock and pain of being deceived again sent me into a tailspin.

"I prayed for the strength to stop acting in such crazy and foolish ways. I began to realize there was no 'greener grass'—but, of course, it was too late.

My husband by that time knew of the affairs and proceeded to file for divorce. This seemed the final blow to an already devastated self-image; but it was only the beginning of the trauma.

I once thought that the hurt before the divorce was the worst I could possibly endure; but I found out that the despair and devastation that follows divorce are indescribable.

By far the most terrible effect of the divorce is knowing my family will never be complete again. Because of my actions, my family has been ripped to shreds. My sons live with my ex-husband in another city, so spending time with them is increasingly difficult. I hate the fact that I will not be there to share the special moments in their lives. My daughter lives with me, but I am beginning to see the adverse effects the divorce has had on her. She is being raised with her dad. Only God know what that is doing to her.

All the wonderful memories, all the precious times as a complete Christian family have become as a vapor, lost in a fog of pain and regret that will remain with me the rest of my life. Having an affair that leads to divorce is like being handed a beautiful bouquet of roses that, once embraced, instantly transforms into a nest of poisonous snakes. An affair does not deal with any problems; it creates worse problems. It is painful and ugly. If suicide were a solution, I would have done it long ago. My only hope now is my relationship with God. He is my restorer and the lifter of my head.

If someone were to tell me that he or she was contemplating divorce, this is the advice I would have.

First, get good Christian counseling. When two people get in the separation and divorce mode, counseling is imperative. Don't bury the issues, but bring them to the surface. Second, bring romance back into your lives. Love is a decision, so make it. Buy each other flowers, and date again. Go out to dinner and talk. Third, forgive one another. Forgiveness is the key to restoration and renewal."

In our vow to "forsake all others," we as men vow to forsake—or give up—all other women for the sake of our new wife. As women you vow to forsake—or give up—all men for the sake of your new husband. We also vow to give up certain rights of privacy and ownership, including the privacy and ownership of our bodies.

We may not realize at first how much we've actually vowed to forsake, but the "forsaking all others" must be owned and grown into if the covenant is going to last. Jesus said in (Matthew 19: 5, 6, NIV), *"For this reason a man will leave his father and mother and be united to his wife, and the two will become one flesh. So they are no longer two, but one. Therefore what God has joined together, let man not separate."*

The failure to forsake others in the marriage covenant could be the greatest cause of divorce. The best marriages in the world—and seasoned married couples will tell you the best marriages occur when the husband and wife have both learned the art of forsaking. Forsaking self and selfish desires are the keys to the success of the marriage covenant (and to life, for that matter).

In the last chapter we discussed honor and dishonor. I said that I believe the opposite of honor is not dishonor, but selfishness. Dishonor always follow selfishness. By focusing on yourself, you always automatically devalue everyone around you—normally, your spouse first.

The ultimate act of selfishness in a marriage covenant is marital infidelity—having an affair. I say that because when affairs take place, no matter how stressed the relationship might be, the perpetrator of the affair has only one thing I mind: getting their "need" met, whatever that might be.

Outside of hunger, the most powerful of all human urges and drives is the sexual appetite.

Any Christian who thinks he or she doesn't need teaching about affair-proofing their marriage is in greater danger than most.

Affairs don't just happen, as anyone who's been there can tell you. We all have certain emotional requirements: love, acceptance, belonging, caring, and tenderness. Our vow is to fulfill those needs within our own marriage. In an affair, there is always a progression. This progression, this gradual straying away, always begins in the emotions. The marriage grows progressively less unified. Fewer needs are met. There is less emotional dependency.

As the person said at the outset of this chapter, the emotional affair began long before the physical affair.

There seem to be four voices that an emotional affair speaks with to lure a person away from the marriage covenant:

1). The voice of pleasure. "Come on, have fun, life is passing you by."

2). The voice of romance. "Someone else cares, someone else is interested, someone else will love you more."

3). The voice of sex. "I'm only interested in the pleasure of the physical act."

4). The voice of ego. "Find someone who can appreciate your mind, personality, and talent."

Now, all marriages need these four areas to remain healthy. But when the voice comes from someone other than our spouse, it is a lying, prowling, deceitful voice; a voice that promises what it can never deliver. The devil is the great counterfeiter and perverter. He always tries to take a good thing that God created, and make it a bad thing.

Affairs always start innocently, the moment you give into the temptation of an affair, the pleasure is gone, and the bondage begins.

In my case, my wife had become ill. The doctors informed us that the illness was terminal. With that news, emotionally it felt as if a light switch had been turned off. Rather than remembering my vow, "in sickness and in health", I chose rather to confide in a divorced woman that I had been counseling. Be assured of this, Satan will always have someone out there who is willing to listen. Someone who he will use to counterfeit the emotions that God intends only for our spouse to meet. After the affair began, my life was overwhelmed with condemnation. Satan reminded me that there could be no bigger hypocrite than myself. A minister called to help marriages, now having an affair myself. The conviction of the Holy Spirit constantly calling me to answer my own alter calls. In the midst of all this craziness, God physically healed my now ex-wife. The lies of the enemy continued to tell me "if you come clean now, you will lose everything!" Without realizing it, I had already lost everything.

No one told me about the guilt and insecurity that would overtake my mind. Romance novels leave out the haunting voices of an affair, the voices that would scream at me in the dark nights and tell me, "It's just a matter of time now before you're caught." No one told me that my affair would leave me tormented. No one told me that this affair that lead to my divorce, would drive me more than once, to suicidal tendencies. But for the grace of God Himself, I am still here. No one—not the soap operas or the grocery stand magazines—bothers to tell you the unutterable downside and destruction of an affair. Maybe that's why affairs are still somewhat appealing to those who haven't yet been destroyed by them.

A famous secular singer wrote in one of his songs, "They would not listen, they're not listening still, perhaps they never will." If you hear anything I have said, please hear this: When your faced with the temptation for an affair, run as fast as you can in the opposite direction. Don't allow an affair to destroy you like it did me.

God has blessed me with five wonderful children. I went from their hero, to their zero. After the divorce and getting the other woman out of my life permanently, it took me five years to restore my relationship with my children. I feel blessed today because I have heard the stories of so many other fathers who were never able to restore their relationships with their families.

Through true repentance and God's unfailing forgiveness, He is able to restore, rebuild and rehabilitate anyone who will submit to His will.

All affairs start with a fantasy. They are fed by a sense of rejection, desperation, and loneliness. The mind becomes the battle ground where this war is to be fought.

The apostle Paul tells us in (2 Corinthians 10:3-5, KJV), *"For though we walk in the flesh, we do not war after the flesh: For the weapons of our warfare are not carnal, but mighty through God to the pulling down of strong holds; casting down imaginations, and every high thing that exalteth itself against the knowledge of God, bringing into captivity every thought to the obedience of Christ."*

God has given us the ability to take captive any thought that tries to parade itself before our lower nature, our flesh. We have the ability to stop the fantasy in the early stages of the thought process. By taking these thoughts captive, they become prisoners—prisoners that must be obedient to the will of Jesus Christ.

Therefore, when you take these thoughts captive to the obedience of Jesus Christ, He frees you from the bondage of those thoughts and handles them Himself. Don't let the fantasy begin. Take the thoughts captive before they destroy you. Don't be so proud, or think you are so strong that this affair won't completely destroy you. Once again, no one is the exception to the rule. If you win the battle of the mind, the affair will never progress.

Probably the most infamous affair recorded in the Scripture was that of King David and Bathsheba, the wife of Uriah. Remember that God called David a man after his own of heart. That should rattle some of you with too much self-confidence. If an affair could take place in a man who God Himself said was after His own heart, then my friend, it could happen to you. Glance at (2 Sam. 11:1-5, NLT)

In the spring of the year, when kings normally go out to war, David sent Joab and the Israelite army to fight the Ammonites. They destroyed the Ammonite army and laid siege to the city of Rabbah. However, David stayed behind in Jerusalem. 2 Late one afternoon, after his midday rest, David got out of bed and was walking on the roof of the palace. As he looked out over the city, he noticed a woman of unusual beauty taking a bath. 3 He sent someone to find out who she was, and he was told, "She is Bathsheba, the daughter of Eliam and the wife of Uriah the Hittite." 4 Then David sent messengers to get her; and when she came to the palace, he slept with her. She had just completed the purification rites after having her menstrual period. Then she returned home. 5 Later, when Bathsheba discovered that she was pregnant, she sent David a message, saying, "I'm pregnant."

Did it really happen that fast? Did David just get up that morning and say to himself, "Today, I commit adultery"? I don't think so. Remember that all affairs are progressive. They start with the innocent meeting at the drinking fountain; the prolonged eye contact with the checker at the grocery store. Small change adds up to unpayable debts as you allow your eye to wander and your tongue to flirt.

Let's track the progression of David's transgression. In 1 Samuel we find that David takes Michal, King Saul's daughter, to be his wife. (1 Samuel 18:20-22, NIV)

20 Now Saul's daughter Michal was in love with David, and when they told Saul about it, he was pleased. 21 "I will give her to him," he thought, "so that she may be a snare to him and so that the hand of the Philistines may be against him." So Saul said to David, "Now you have a second opportunity to become my son-in-law."

22 Then Saul ordered his attendants: "Speak to David privately and say, 'Look, the king likes you, and his attendants all love you; now become his son-in-law.'"

So the wedding took place. Michal was madly in love with David and probably vice-versa. But David liked to travel, so he wasn't there to meet the needs of his new wife like she had always dreamed of, and eventually some bitterness began to set in. After bitterness came resentment, maybe even from the fact that David was always getting attention and no one really noticed Michal (or as she was known as "David's wife").

The story progresses and David goes to recapture the ark of the covenant that had been stolen by the Philistines. He rejoices greatly as the ark is brought back into Israel. Now we can see the bitterness and resentment begin to surface:

(2 Samuel 6:12-23, NIV)

12 Now King David was told, "The Lord has blessed the household of Obed-Edom and everything he has, because of the ark of God." So David went to bring up the ark of God from the house of Obed-Edom to the City of David with rejoicing. 13 When those who were carrying the ark of the Lord had taken six steps, he sacrificed a bull and a fattened calf. 14 Wearing a linen ephod, David was dancing before the Lord with all his might, 15 while he and all Israel were bringing up the ark of the Lord with shouts and the sound of trumpets. 16 As the ark of the Lord was entering the City of David, Michal daughter of Saul watched from a window. And when she saw King David leaping and dancing before the Lord, she despised him in her heart. 17 They brought the ark of the Lord and set it in its place inside the tent that David had pitched for it, and David sacrificed burnt offerings and fellowship offerings before the Lord. 18 After he had finished sacrificing the burnt offerings and fellowship offerings, he blessed the people in the name of the Lord Almighty. 19 Then he gave a loaf of bread, a cake of dates and a cake of raisins to each person in the whole crowd of

Israelites, both men and women. And all the people went to their homes. 20 When David returned home to bless his household, Michal daughter of Saul came out to meet him and said, "How the king of Israel has distinguished himself today, going around half-naked in full view of the slave girls of his servants as any vulgar fellow would!" 21 David said to Michal, "It was before the Lord, who chose me rather than your father or anyone from his house when he appointed me ruler over the Lord's people Israel—I will celebrate before the Lord. 22 I will become even more undignified than this, and I will be humiliated in my own eyes. But by these slave girls you spoke of, I will be held in honor." 23 And Michal daughter of Saul had no children to the day of her death.

Can you feel it? Can you recognize it? The temperature of David and Michal's marriage. Have you ever felt this in your own marriage? She is extremely bitter and hurt over the lack of communication; she feels that her father has been dishonored by her husband. Have you ever said dishonoring things to your spouse about your in-laws? What's David feeling? Probably rejection from his wife. He comes home hoping to have her rejoice with him over the fact that the ark has been returned, only to find her despising him. He must have felt loneliness, by this time, having been gone for so long.

Now those voices, that needed to be taken captive, began to speak to him. The voices that have been the downfall and the destruction of thousands of men before him, and thousands after him. The voices of an affair begin to taunt him over the course of the weeks that follow, and then he walks out onto his balcony one spring morning.

(2 Samuel 11:1-9, NIV)

In the spring, at the time when kings go off to war, David sent Joab out with the king's men and the whole Israelite army. They destroyed the Ammonites and besieged Rabbah. But David remained in Jerusalem. 2 One evening David got up from his bed and walked around on the roof of the palace. From the roof he saw a woman bathing. The woman was very beautiful, 3 and David sent someone to find out about her. The man said, "She is Bathsheba, the daughter of Eliam and the wife of Uriah the Hittite." 4 Then David sent messengers to get her. She came to him, and he slept with her. (Now she was purifying herself from her monthly uncleanness.) Then she went back home. 5 The woman conceived and sent word to David, saying, "I am pregnant."

6 So David sent this word to Joab: "Send me Uriah the Hittite." And Joab sent him to David. 7 When

Uriah came to him, David asked him how Joab was, how the soldiers were and how the war was going. 8 Then David said to Uriah, "Go down to your house and wash your feet." So Uriah left the palace, and a gift from the king was sent after him. 9 But Uriah slept at the entrance to the palace with all his master's servants and did not go down to his house.

That morning the voice of pleasure might have spoken to David and said, "Don't waste your life with Michal. You're the king! Bathsheba would be much more fun." The voice of romance chimed in and said "Bathsheba would care about you more, she would love you more, surely she would be interested in the things that you are." About that time the voice of sex said, "You know, Davie, the action hasn't been too great around home lately. Just look how hot Bathsheba is. She can satisfy you."

Then the voice of ego finished him off. "At least Bathsheba would respect you David. She would appreciate you for your ability to be a great warrior. You know she thinks you're talented. You ought to go for the gusto, David!"

Listen, if you can't take care of the grass you have now, you sure won't be able to take care of someone else's. This passage perfectly illustrates the progression of an affair.

1). You're in a place you shouldn't be (v. 1)

2). You begin to look at what you shouldn't (v. 2).

3). You begin to say things you shouldn't (v. 3-4a).

4). You begin to do things you shouldn't (v. 4b-5).

5). You try to cover up your sin with more sin (v. 6-9)

When any friendship with the opposite sex begins to threaten what we hold dear—our relationship with God, our spouse, and our children—what do we do? Run! Run! Run! Get away from that situation! Then talk with a godly friend of the same sex about your temptation. Ask yourself why you are being lured away from your covenant relationship. Who is behind it? Chances are, you'll find the devil lurking there. The grass may appear greener on the other side of the fence, but remember, that grass still has to be mowed and watered. The Bible tells us to draw from the well of life: the word of God.

(Proverbs 3:7, NIV)

Do not be wise in your own eyes; fear the Lord and shun evil.

Realize that trying to handle an affair on your own

will cost you everything. Get some help. Talk to someone else about it immediately, otherwise it will continue to be a phantom in your mind and emotions.

One of the best ways to "Forsake all others", is to memorize (2 Corinthians 10:3-5). Take captive every thought that tries to come against the knowledge of God. God really has given you a supernatural weapon to defeat the enemy when you're tempted by an affair. Your mind controlled by the word of God.

CHAPTER EIGHT

"FORSAKING ALL OTHERS..."
(Part 2)

Let's look at something unpleasant: The consequences of failing to "forsake all others." Listen to the writer of Proverbs:
(Proverbs 5:1-14, NIV)
My son, pay attention to my wisdom,
  turn your ear to my words of insight,
2 that you may maintain discretion
  and your lips may preserve knowledge.
3 For the lips of the adulterous woman drip honey,
  and her speech is smoother than oil;
4 but in the end she is bitter as gall,
  sharp as a double-edged sword.

5 Her feet go down to death;
*   her steps lead straight to the grave.*
6 She gives no thought to the way of life;
*   her paths wander aimlessly, but she does not know it.*
7 Now then, my sons, listen to me;
*   do not turn aside from what I say.*
8 Keep to a path far from her,
*   do not go near the door of her house,*
9 lest you lose your honor to others
*   and your dignity to one who is cruel,*
10 lest strangers feast on your wealth
*   and your toil enrich the house of another.*
11 At the end of your life you will groan,
*   when your flesh and body are spent.*
12 You will say, "How I hated discipline!
*   How my heart spurned correction!*
13 I would not obey my teachers
*   or turn my ear to my instructors.*
14 And I was soon in serious trouble
*   in the assembly of God's people."*

What takes place in the aftermath of an affair? Even more important, how can a marriage be saved after an affair? Research has found that there are four types of marriages that are more vulnerable to an affair. Before we look at these four types, we need to be reminded that all marriages are vulnerable to affairs. Anytime a couple comes to a place where they feel it could never happen to them, they are standing in the threshold of failure. Never, never let your guard down. Our marriages must be protected. We need to build hedges around them.

While traveling in Eastern Europe a few years ago, our outreach team visited some of the lavish palaces that were once occupied by the Czars of those nations. Those palaces contained more beauty than anything I had ever seen. Some of their ceilings were created from solid gold. Their walls were decorated with original paintings from the most well-known artists that have ever lived: Monet, Picasso, Rembrandt. With the wealth these castles contained, I wondered how many people through the years wanted to break in and steal the works of art.

Surely they had gates of steel, fences made of solid iron, I thought. As I went outside I was surprised to find no steel gates or even iron fences, but hedges. Thick bushy hedges that were loaded with big long thorns. Some of the hedges were at least 20 feet thick. It would have taken days for someone to penetrate the walls of thorns.

Thorny hedges are what we need around our marriages. Hedges will allow us to protect the valuable assets of our marriage. Hedges will give us the time to defend our marriages when any perpetrator decides they would like to go where they don't belong. Today, I am happily in my second and final marriage. After seven years of being divorced and making the decision that I would no longer date, I would put my energy in simply serving the Lord. But then I met my wife. It was Father's day and four of my five children had come to take me to lunch. As we strolled through the quaint little shops in Murphy's California, I met Christy. I can honestly say it seemed like God had placed a spot light on her in the middle of this shop where she worked. Today I do not believe that it was an accident that most of my children were there the day I met my new wife. In this chapter I hope to give you seed for hedges that will grow a wall of protection around the most sacred of possessions, your marriage covenant.

Today, Christy and I have planted thick hedges around our marriage covenant. One of the hedges that I have planted today is that I no longer do counseling with women in my office alone. If a woman comes to my office for counseling and her husband refuses to come, I will ask one of our female assistants to sit in the session with us. The rule is this: If two is company, three is security.

There are at least four types of marriages that fail to grow hedges of protection, or have simply allowed the hedges they once had to die.

1). Intimacy avoidance.

These are marriages where both partners keep one another at arm's length. There is no emotional closeness; their souls rarely touch. Sadly, it is possible for a married couple to never experience their souls touching.

There is an intimacy available to born-again Christian couples that will allow them to communicate from the heart and not just the mouth. It comes from the eyes, which are the windows to the soul, not just the actions. In my years of counseling I have found so many marriages void of true intimacy. The couples are like a pair of windshield wipers. They always go in the same direction but they always keep their distance, never touching. Then one day someone shows up and does touch the soul, and an affair is ignited.

2). Conflict avoidance.

This may be the type of affair that Christian couples are most vulnerable to. This is a marriage where one or both people in the marriage feel that everything has to look perfect; that it's wrong to have any emotional ups and downs. Their marriage is similar to a dial tone—assuring at first, but the longer you listen to it, the more annoying it becomes.

Troubling issues are rarely addressed, but rather stuffed away in hopes they will disappear. Then one day someone not so boring shows up, and the affair ignites.

The flames of an affair are similar to a "wild fire." In the part of California where I lived, wild fires plagued our foothills every summer. Fire fighters from all over the nation were called to put them out. Inevitably, as one is put out, another one started.

Wild fires and affairs have three ingredients in common. Dry material, oxygen, and a spark.

In an affair, the Christian person has become spiritually dry. Church has become boring—much like their marriage. The Bible refuses to come to life, and their prayer life doesn't exist.

The oxygen—or fuel—of an affair is in the intimate glance or conversation with the person who has found little interest in their own marriage relationship.

The spark is when the two tell one another how they feel about each other. The three ingredients add up to a sinful combustion that burns everything in its path. Nothing is off limits for destruction. An affair destroys everything!

3). The empty nest affair.

This is the affair that takes place after 20 or 30 years of marriage, when a couple feels they have achieved their purpose. Their children are raised and now they realize they have invested their life into their kids, but not into each other. One day they look at each other—and don't even know one another. They begin to look for emotional satisfaction elsewhere. The void they find in their lives lead them into the arms of another.

4). The "Out the door" marriage.

These are the people that regretted marrying their spouse from day one. After the children are raised, they are out the door. Sometimes these affairs are planned for years, subconsciously, to sabotage the marriage.

The devastation of an affair to both the victim and the scoundrel are very similar. Both the husband and the wife experience real grief, comparable only to the grief experienced in the death of a loved one. The grief they both feel is real. It's real because there actually has been a death. The death was intimacy. The pain for both is tremendous.

All affairs can be avoided, including the four types that were just mentioned, if the couple will see that there is one ingredient always present in their marriage: intimacy. True intimacy with your spouse is the best hedge you can build.

Several years ago we started hosting weekend marriage conferences, *(for more information on these conferences please see the contact information at the end of this book).* The Lord has taught us how born-again couples can have true intimacy in their marriage. Intimacy that enables the couple to touch the chords of their spouse's spirit in harmony with everything they are made of.

This intimacy was lost in the Garden of Eden with Adam and Eve, in their relationship with one another and with God. This type of intimacy the Bible calls "yada." Yada is the Hebrew word for the deepest kind of intimacy. When a couple has this type of intimacy—and it's available to any born-again Christian—the spirit of divorce is destroyed.

We have heard testimony after testimony of couples that were on their way to divorce or had completely given up on having a true intimate relationship. God, through this conference has changed their lives.

It's been said, "We become intimate to whom we pray , and with whom we pray," Praying with your spouse births intimacy. I have yet to counsel any couple that has been divorced—or even contemplated it—and who also told me they had a great prayer life.

In Ephesians chapter 6, the apostle Paul records one of the best know passages regarding spiritual warfare. We know this passage as the application of our spiritual armor. The helmet, the breast plate, the sword of the Spirit, etc. But— follow me, here—Paul opens Ephesians chapter six as an instruction on relationships. He places side by side two teachings: one on prayer, the other on relationships and marriage. I don't think this was coincidental. Paul had discovered that prayer and right relationships equal intimacy. His final instruction was this: (Ephesians 6:18, NIV). *18 And pray in the Spirit on all occasions with all kinds of prayers and requests. With this in mind, be alert and always keep on praying for all the Lord's people.*

Pray for all the Lord's people? It doesn't sound like "counseling talk," but it makes a marriage work a whole lot better.

The woman that Jesus met at the well at Sychar had more of an unmet need than just water. She had a severe intimacy deficiency. Jesus told her, *"If you continue to drink of the water you've been drinking, you'll thirst again, but if you drink of the water that I offer you, you'll never thirst again."* Her reply was, give me some of that water! And Jesus' response to her may have seemed strange but in reality He saw exactly what she needed.

She needed an intimacy injection. She needed intimacy with God, and intimacy in her marriage relationship.

(John 4:15-18, NIV)

15 The woman said to him, "Sir, give me this water so that I won't get thirsty and have to keep coming here to draw water." 16 He told her, "Go, call your husband and come back." 17 "I have no husband," she replied. Jesus said to her, "You are right when you say you have no husband. 18 The fact is, you have had five husbands, and the man you now have is not your husband. What you have just said is quite true."

This woman had gone from man to man in search of intimacy, and found none. She had gone from failed relationship to failed relationship. And she was still searching. How do I know that? Because satisfied partners don't wander!

In Kevin Leman's book "Keeping Your Family Together when the World is Falling Apart" (Delacorte Press), he speaks of a television show that pitted fidelity versus infidelity. One 80-year-old lady stood up and told how she and her husband had experienced over 50 years of marital happiness, without any infidelity. When asked how they did it, her response caused the audience to roar. She said: "I got all the juices out of him and didn't leave any for anyone else." People laughed with her, because they knew her words were filled with wisdom.

If marriage partners are getting enough attention, affection, and intimacy at home, they're not likely to stray into an affair. In Leman's book, there is a graphic description of intimacy that dies of sheer neglect, in a poem entitled

The Wall:
"Their wedding picture mocked them from the table, these two whose minds no longer touched. They lived with such a heavy barricade between them that neither battering ram of words nor artilleries of touch could break it down. Somewhere, between the oldest child's first tooth and the youngest daughter's graduation, they lost each other.
Throughout the years each slowly unraveled a tangled ball of string called self,

And as they tugged at stubborn knots, each hid
their searching from the other.
Sometimes she cried at night and begged the
whispering darkness to tell her who she really
was.
He would lay beside her, snoring like a hibernating
bear, totally unaware of her winter.
Once, after they had made love, he wanted so
badly to tell her how afraid he was of dying, but,
fearing to show his naked soul, he spoke instead
about the beauty of her breasts.
She took a course in modern art, trying to find
herself in colors splashed upon a canvas,
complaining to other women about men who are
so insensitive.
He climbed into a tomb called "the office,"
wrapped his mind in a shroud of paper figures,
and buried himself in customers.
Slowly, the wall between them rose, cemented by
the mortar of indifference.
One day, reaching out to touch each other,
they found a barrier they could not penetrate,
and recoiling from the coldness of the stone,
each retreated from the stranger on the other
side.
For when love dies, it does not die in a moment of
angry battle,
Nor does it die when two fiery bodies lose their

heat.
It lies panting, exhausted, dying at the bottom of a wall it could no longer scale."

Whether or not an affair has taken place in your marriage, each of us could use an "intimacy injection."

How can that take place?

1). At a time when the two of you will not be disturbed, ask one another, "How would you define intimacy?" Then listen to what your spouse says. If we are honest with one another, we will list our unmet needs of intimacy.

2). Pray with one another on a regular basis. I know it's difficult, I know it takes extra time, but we must make it an area of priority in order to build intimacy and grow hedges. Pray with your spouse sometimes before you make love. Inviting the presence of God into our marriage bed makes all the difference in the world.

3). Every once in a while, change your schedule. You need time as a couple to your selves—even away from your children. There will come a day when they are grown and gone. Invest in your spouse now.

4). Talk to your pastor about bringing our marriage conference to your church. They are not expensive, and it will make rough marriages smooth, and good marriages great. We can all improve our relationships.

CHAPTER NINE

"TILL DEATH SHOULD PART US..."

When God gave Israel the choice of "the covenant or the curse," there were no misunderstandings as to the seriousness of the matter. Israel knew that a blood covenant had severe consequences if broken. The word "everlasting and eternal" was frequently used when this type of covenant was established.

The vows that we made to one another in our marriage covenant stated that we vowed to stay together "until death should part us." The passage of scripture this book has been based on is (Malachi 2:1-8, NIV)

"And now, you priests, this warning is for you. 2 If you do not listen, and if you do not resolve to honor my name," says the Lord Almighty, "I will send a curse on you, and I will curse your blessings. Yes, I have already cursed them, because you have not resolved to honor me.

3 "Because of you I will rebuke your descendants[a]; I will smear on your faces the dung from your festival sacrifices, and you will be carried off with it. 4 And you will know that I have sent you this warning so that my covenant with Levi may continue," says the Lord Almighty. 5 "My covenant was with him, a covenant of life and peace, and I gave them to him; this called for reverence and he revered me and stood in awe of my name. 6 True instruction was in his mouth and nothing false was found on his lips. He walked with me in peace and uprightness, and turned many from sin. 7 "For the lips of a priest ought to preserve knowledge, because he is the messenger of the Lord Almighty and people seek instruction from his mouth. 8 But you have turned from the way and by your teaching have caused many to stumble; you have violated the covenant with Levi," says the Lord Almighty.

As we bring these chapters to a close, it's safe to say that divorce causes death. The words "until death should part us" weren't just romantic poetry. They were true—and are true—in a physical sense. When divorce enters the picture, the process of death quickly accelerates. This may not be evident in the physical sense until years down the road; but in the relational and spiritual sense, and in the family, death sets in immediately.

"One man with one woman for life.
That's the covenant."

Divorce kills the opportunity to enjoy our children and raise them in a balanced relationship. Probably the most extensive study done to date on the effects of divorced in men, women, and children, is the book "Second Chances" by Judith S. Wallerstein (Houghton Miffin, Press)

Wallerstein's book traced 60 divorced families for the past 20 years, through every stage—from the separation of the couple, to raising the children in broken homes, then the common second and often third divorces.

Her findings are frightening, and she concludes her 300-page book by saying this: "Divorce is a wrenching experience for many adults and almost all children. It is almost always more devastating for children than for their parents. Divorce is not an event that stands alone in children's or adults' experience. It is a continuation that begins in the unhappy marriage and extends through the separation, the divorce, and any remarriages and second divorces.

The effects of divorce are often long-lasting. Children are especially affected because divorce occurs during their formative years. What they see and experience becomes a part of their inner world, their view of themselves, and their view of society. Almost all children of divorce regard their childhood and adolescence as having taken place in the shadow of divorce. They feel they had to suffer from their parents' mistakes.

In this study, half of the children entered adulthood as worried, underachieving, self-deprecating, and sometimes angry young men and women. Some felt used in a battle that was never their own. Others felt deprived of the parenting and family protection that they always wanted and never got.

Finally, and perhaps most important for society, the cumulative effect of the failing marriage and divorce rose to a crescendo as each child entered adulthood. It was here, as these young men and women faced the developmental task of establishing love and intimacy, that they most felt the lack of an example for a loving, enduring, and moral relationship between a man and a woman.

We are raising a large segment of our society

of young people, without the ability to have a healthy, normal, loving, intimate relationship with the opposite sex, simply because they have never seen it modeled in the home.

Divorce is killing families, and it must stop. The body of Christ is the vessel that God desires to pour Himself into. There is no other model. Divorce is killing hopes and dreams and destinies that will never be realized.

(John 10:10, NIV)

The thief comes only to steal and kill and destroy; I have come that they may have life, and have it to the full.

When I read that, I hear a voice in my mind. The voice is coming from a married couple of happiness past, and it says, "I don't know if I even love you anymore. I don't know if I can ever trust you again." And for the first time in a long time, this couple agrees on something.

They agree that they used to believe that John 10:10 was meant for their marriage. They used to believe that God's plan for their lives and their marriage was *"a life more abundant, and a life more full."* But now all they see is the pain and the storms that life has brought, and the toll on their marriage. Yes, they want to believe that's still God's plan for their life, but all they see is the wreckage and despair of what once was.

Maybe that voice I heard was actually mine. But maybe that voice you hear is yours. And now you have a question. "What do we do now? What do we do with this shipwreck?"

The Bible records an account of a shipwreck—a shipwreck that the apostle Paul found himself right in the middle of. Inside this literal account of Paul's shipwreck, lies the answer for our shipwrecked marriages.

The story opened with the apostle Paul being held on a ship with 276 people. They failed to heed the instructions of the Lord through Paul and found themselves in the midst of very violent storm. In (Acts 27:20, NIV), we can get a feel for how the people felt: *When neither sun nor stars appeared for many days and the storm continued raging, we finally gave up all hope of being saved.*

People at the point of divorce have been so beaten by the storms of life that they finally give up all hope of saving their marriage. I want to close these chapters with four things we must do if we ever find our marriages at the point of divorce.

(Acts 27:21-25, NIV)
[21] After they had gone a long time without food, Paul stood up before them and said: "Men, you should have taken my advice not to sail from Crete; then you would have spared yourselves this

damage and loss. ²² But now I urge you to keep up your courage, because not one of you will be lost; only the ship will be destroyed. ²³ Last night an angel of the God to whom I belong and whom I serve stood beside me ²⁴ and said, 'Do not be afraid, Paul. You must stand trial before Caesar; and God has graciously given you the lives of all who sail with you.' ²⁵ So keep up your courage, men, for I have faith in God that it will happen just as he told me.

The first thing you need to do if you find your marriage in spiritual shipwreck is, get around someone who's heard from God. Get away from the people who say, "Yeah, your spouse is nothing but a bum, you can do much better than him or her." Paul tells these people, "Don't be afraid, I've heard from God, and if God says we're going to make it, we are going to make it." I imagine there were plenty of grumblers and commiserators on that ship, but none of them had a solution. Sometimes we get so weak that it becomes difficult to hope for anything by ourselves.

Find someone who will agree with you for the salvation of your marriage. The Bible teaches us that if two of us agree in faith on anything that is in the will of God, God will answer that prayer. (1 John 5:14, 15, NIV)

¹⁴ This is the confidence we have in approaching

God: that if we ask anything according to his will, he hears us. ¹⁵ And if we know that he hears us— whatever we ask—we know that we have what we asked of him.

Find someone that will stand with you for your marriage and your family.

Secondly, if you find your marriage in a shipwreck, stay with the ship.

(Acts 27:30, 31, NIV)

³⁰ In an attempt to escape from the ship, the sailors let the lifeboat down into the sea, pretending they were going to lower some anchors from the bow. ³¹ Then Paul said to the centurion and the soldiers, "Unless these men stay with the ship, you cannot be saved."

The English author, John Mortimer, wrote a book called *Clinging to the Wreckage*. He said the title came to him one day as he was having lunch with an experienced yachtsman. He asked the yachtsman, "Isn't it dangerous sailing the ocean as a sport?" The man's answer shocked him. "No, not if you never learn to swim." You see when you're in trouble out in the ocean and you know how to swim, it's inevitable that you will attempt to swim toward shore. You'll almost always drown. My advice to you is the same: Cling to the wreckage. It is almost always better to start with what you have and build, or rebuild, than to abandon what you have and swim for shore.

Every marriage, however poor, has something to build on. Every marriage has had its share of special feelings, sentimental occasions, and intimate moments. They may have been few and far between recently, and they may seem remote under the pains and agonies of a deteriorating relationship, but they are there nevertheless, and they form a much more solid launch pad for the future than an untried or broken relationship. In order to save our marriages and our families, we have to stay on board.

Third, recognize that your marriage needs nourishment.

(Acts 27:34, NIV)

"Now I urge you to take some food. You need it to survive. Not one of you will lose a single hair from his head."

What's the food of marriage? Intimacy fed through prayer. I am not referring to little Band-Aid prayers we pray when we find ourselves in trouble.   "God-won't-you-please-mend-my-marriage?"

I'm referring to prayers that touch the throne room of God; intercession that empties you before God so that God can once again become the center of your family and your life. These are the prayers that recognize there is something wrong with "my" life, and prayers that tell God, "I'm surrendering my will to you in order for you to not only come in, but to take over!"

It doesn't take a genius to figure that at least half our marital problems are our fault, not our mate's. Very few marriages go bad because one partner is a scoundrel and the other is a saint. The place to begin working on a faulty marriage, therefore, is always in the self, never in the other person or the situation.

We start the process by telling God, with all honesty, "I'm yours to do with as you see fit." You will breed an intimacy with Him like you've never known, and this will draw you close to your spouse.

Fourth, get away from the circumstances that are causing your marriage to fail.
(Acts 27:40, NIV)

Cutting loose the anchors, they left them in the sea and at the same time untied the ropes that held the rudders. Then they hoisted the foresail to the wind and made for the beach.

What anchors are dragging your marriage down? Many times they are anchors of un-repented sin. For the salvation of your marriage covenant, What is the right thing to do? Listen, doing the right thing is rarely the "easy" thing to do, but, doing the right thing is always right to do.

Ask yourself once again, what is God's will for my marriage? If we removed the selfish desires of just the things your flesh wants, what does God want? I can almost guarantee you that He does not want this divorce. He wants reconciliation between you and the spouse of your youth according to the prophet Malachi.

(Hebrews 12:1, 2, NIV)

Therefore, since we are surrounded by such a great cloud of witnesses, let us throw off everything that hinders and the sin that so easily entangles. And let us run with perseverance the race marked out for us, ² fixing our eyes on Jesus, the pioneer and perfecter of faith. For the joy set before him he endured the cross, scorning its shame, and sat down at the right hand of the throne of God.

What anchors are weighing down and destroying your marriage? They may be anchors of unhealthy friendships, anchors of emotional or even physical affairs, maybe your anchor is selfishness. Your anchor may be something that you've been in bondage to for years. God is willing and able to break that bondage for the sake of your marriage covenant, if you're willing to cut that rope.

In review:

1). Find someone who's heard from God to encourage you.

2). Stay with the ship.

3). Nourish your marriage through prayer and intimacy.

4). Cut loose the anchors that are destroying your marriage.

Wait! You know what? I hear that voice again. This time it's saying: "I've done all that Tom and my life is still falling apart!" Let's look what happened to Paul at the end of this story. God said their ship was going to wreck, and it did. (Acts 27:41-44, NIV)

41 But the ship struck a sandbar and ran aground. The bow stuck fast and would not move, and the stern was broken to pieces by the pounding of the surf. 42 The soldiers planned to kill the prisoners to prevent any of them from swimming away and escaping. 43 But the centurion wanted to spare Paul's life and kept them from carrying out their plan. He ordered those who could swim to jump overboard first and get to land. 44 The rest were to get there on planks or on other pieces of the ship. In this way everyone reached land safely.

God promised every one of them that He would deliver them to safety—just like He promises us. A "broken piece of ship" may be the only thing that you have to hold on to in your marriage. May I remind you that God loves to use broken things? You are more useful to Him broken than "fixed," because in our normal "fixed" condition we don't recognize our dependence on God.

My friend, you can take my advice and learn from my sin and mistakes and not destroy everything that God has blessed you with, or you can choose your own path and learn divorced lessons on your own. I will remind you one more time before we close this chapter, divorce is a cruel instructor.

If all you have to hold on to is that broken piece of a marriage, it's that broken piece that God will use to restore the covenant. Let it become the first plank in a new home. Let Him use your past experience as a foundation for a glorious future.

You can make it! You can keep the vows you've made to God, if you're willing. You don't have to live under the curse that follows all divorces. God has given each of us the ministry of reconciliation. Remember, He is not a respecter of persons. He wants your marriage to be blessed. I close by reminding each of us of the vows we made to one another and to God.

"I take you to be my wedded spouse, to have and to hold, from this day forward, for better or for worse, for richer or for poorer, in sickness and in health, to love and to honor, forsaking all others, until death should part us."

"What God has joined together,
let no one put asunder."
Amen.

ABOUT THE AUTHOR

Tom Smith and his wife Christy are Pastors of "Family Strong" the marriage and family ministry at The House, Modesto, CA. (Senior Pastors, Glen and Deborah Berteau). Tom is an author and popular conference speaker in the United States and abroad. True intimacy with God and one another is at the forefront of their ministry. You will enjoy his entertaining style as well as be challenged to reach for that intimate relationship you've always dreamed of.

You can reach Pastor Tom Smith at:
Email: strongmarriages@yahoo.com

For other books and ministry material please visit:
Website: Tomsmithministry.com

Made in the USA
Las Vegas, NV
26 October 2024

10456604R00075